SPANISH WORKBOOK

EASY SPANISH PHRASE FOR EVERYONE

Introduction To Spanish For Beginners With Commonly Spoken Spanish Phrases and How To Talk Spanish

MARELI GUTIERREZ

Table of Contents

Section 1: Vocabulary and Grammar

The Basics

The Alphabet and Common Notations

Learning the Spanish alphabet is easy as it is the same as the English alphabet, with one new letter and a few extra markings floating around for emphasis. The first mark is called a tilde (~), which you will sometimes see appear over the letter N, making it become Ñ, which makes a sound that is somewhere between the letters N and Y. Ñ is the only new letter you must learn here.

You will see it used in words such as the following:

Spanish	español
Boy/girl	el niño / la niña
Mountain	la montaña
Dream	el sueño

The other marks you will see floating around are the accent marks, which are floating little dashes that will sometimes appear over vowels. This mark is there to tell you which part of the word is stressed. Put another way, it tells you which syllable has the most emphasis when you pronounce it. Technically every word in both the Spanish and English language has a syllable that is stressed. This small change in pronunciation can really change your sentence.

- ¿Donde esta mi Pa**pá**?
  Where is my Dad?

- ¿Donde esta mi **Pa**pa?
  Where is my Potato?

You will notice that the word for potato does not carry any visible accent mark, but it does have a stressed syllable. This is because the Spanish language has a set of rules that tell you when to write it, and when to leave it unmarked. The rules can get technical, and they are worth learning as you explore the Spanish language. However, do not worry too much yet. Simply know that these are markings that can change your pronunciation, and therefore create new words. We will cover the rules for accents at a later point in this book.

Pronouncing Ls and Rs

Repeating Ls do make a Y sound.

- Amarillo (Yellow), Llamame (Call me)

Spanish has a distinct rolling R sound. If you are new to making this noise, say the following words out loud in English:

Water – Butter – City – Leader.

There is a moment in each of these words where your tongue will tap along the roof of your mouth in a very quick and brief way. These words each have a single tap, but the rolling R is a series of taps done in the same breath.

Try practicing this sound by saying those four words over and over.

Unfortunately, you do not always roll the R, as exciting as this new sound might be.

The following instances require the rolling R:

When you see a word that starts with an R.

- El Rincon (corner), El Raton (mouse)

When the word has two R's.

- Correr (Run), Carro (Expensive)

When the letter appears immediately after an L, M, N, S, X, or Z.

- Sonrisa (smile)

Pronouncing Vowels and Vowel Groupings

Vowels are shorter and generally unchanging in Spanish. Variety emerges when you look at vowel groupings and how words are separated into distinct syllables.

A is pronounced as the 'a' in "Law" or "Father".

E is pronounced as the 'e' in "Set" or "Fred".

I is pronounced as the 'ea' in "Eat" or the 'ee' in "See".

O is pronounced as the 'o' in "phone" or "no".

U is pronounced as the u in "flute" or "tune".

Y is treated as the letter 'i' when it is in a vowel grouping.

Diphthongs

Diphthongs are formed when you put together a strong vowel (A, E, or O) with a weak vowel (I or U), or when you place two weak vowels together. This combination of vowels creates a new sound.

There is a long list of possible combinations for different pairs of vowels, and this might seem to be a lot to take in. However, if you keep in mind which vowels are strong and which are weak, just remember to stress the stronger vowel and just merge the same vowel noises as before.

AU – 'ow' sound	el autor (author)
AI or AY– long I sound	aire (air), hay (there is)
EU – 'ehoo' sound	la deuda (debt)
EI or EY – long A sound	la reina (queen), la ley (law)
IA – 'yah' sound	estudiar (to study)
IE – 'yeh' sound	el viento (wind)
IO – 'yoh' sound	delicioso (delicious)

IU – 'you' sound — la ciudad (city)

OI or OY – 'oy' sound — oigo (I hear), hoy (today)

UA – 'wah' sound — el agua (water)

UE – 'weh' sound — el juego (game)

UI – 'wee' sound — el ruido (noise), muy (very)

UO – 'woh' sound — antiguo (old)

Hiatuses

These are vowel groupings that look very similar to the diphthongs, but they are pronounced in separate syllables. This happens when you have two strong vowels next to each other, or when a weak vowel has an accent over it.

One example you may have seen comes in the form of common names: Mario and María. Notice how Ma-rio is a two-syllable name with a diphthong, and Ma-rí-a is a three syllable name with a hiatus instead. The accent over the 'i' transforms the weak vowel into a strong vowel that has its own emphasis, which in turn has the effect of creating a separate syllable.

AÍ – ah-EE — la raíz (root), el paraíso (paradise)

AÚ – ah-OO — el baúl (trunk), el ataúd (coffin)

OÍ – oh-EE — oír (hearing), egoísta (selfish)

EÍ – eh-EE — la cafeína (caffeine)

EÚ – eh-OO — reúno (gathered)

ÍA – EE-ah — dormía (they slept), corría (they ran)

ÍE – EE-eh — sonríe (smile), el resfríe (the common cold)

ÍO – EE-oh — frío (cold), mío (mine)

ÚA – OO-ah	Evaluar (Evaluate)
ÚE – OO-eh	gradúe (graduated), tatúe (to tattoo)
ÚO – OO-oh	continúo (continuous)
AE – ah-eh	caer (to fall), traer (to bring)
AO – ah-oh	el cacao (cocoa), el caos (chaos)
AA – ah-ah	contraargumento (counter argument)
EA – eh-ah	el teatro (theater), la aldea (village)
EO – eh-oh	paseo (walk), deseo (desire)
EE – eh-eh	leer (to read), creer (to believe)
OA – oh-ah	la canoa (canoe), el coautor (co-author)
OE – oh-eh	el poeta (poet), el héroe (hero)
OO – oh-oh	cooperar (cooperate)

Silent H

The Spanish language usually does not assign a sound that is specific to the letter h. If you have been going through the examples above and adding a breathy 'h' sound, try the examples again without it. This letter normally takes a silent role in words like Hormiga (ant) and hombre (man).

The letter H still plays three major roles:

1. Paired with the letter 'c', you get the familiar 'ch' sound.

El chico/La chica	Boy/Girl
chulo	Cool/Cute
El techo	Roof
La cuchara	Spoon

2. Synonyms!

A (to/at/of)	Ha (has/have)
Hola (hello)	Ola (ocean wave)
Honda (deep)	Onda (ocean wave)
Hasta (until)	Asta (flagpole)

3. Separating vowel groupings into extra syllables.

In the case of vowel groupings, this silent letter has the same effect you see in hiatuses. When it is placed between two vowels that might be read as a single syllable diphthong sound, the sound is broken down to two syllables. Put another way: even though the letter h has no sound of its own, it does have the ability to break a word into extra syllables when it is placed between some vowels.

Here are some examples.

AHO	ahorrar (to save up)
UHO	el búho (owl)
AHI	cahída (the fall)
EHI	el vehículo (vehicle)
OHO	el alcohol (alcohol)
OHI	prohíbe (prohibit)

Conjugations

Several words will need more study than others simply because they exist in various forms. These words are important to practice because you will stand out like a sore thumb if you do not know how to use them. This can be the equivalent of hearing a person say "I am exciting" when they talk about looking forward to a party you are planning. You assume they are telling you that they are 'excited' to attend, but there is always a chance that they are simply bragging about their 'wow factor'. Conjugations help you communicate more clearly, and they help you speak the language fluently.

Verbs change form based on the situation they are being used for. This means that you must know WHO is taking the action and WHEN the action is taking place. This is just as true for English as it is for Spanish. You know the difference between he took, she will take, and they have taken. You know when to use find vs found, fight vs fought, and buy vs bought. With the following fundamentals, and plenty of practice, you will be able to know the difference in Spanish as well.

It is important to know what the infinitive form of a word is and how this impacts the conjugation of all other forms of the word. Infinitives are the base word that is unconjugated. This will always be a single word and it will end in either -ar, -er, or -ir.

Camin**ar** (to walk), beb**er** (to drink), escrib**ir** (to write)

You can begin to conjugate once you have:

1. The infinitive form of the word.

2. The WHO that is taking the action.

Yo	I/Me
Tú	You (informal/friendly)
Usted	You (formal/respectful)
Él/Ella	Him/Her
Nosotros/as	We/Us
Vosotros/as	You, plural (informal, only in Spain)
Ustedes	You, plural
Ellos/Ellas	They or Them

3. The WHEN of the same action.

Past tense, present tense, future tense.

-ar Verbs, Present Tense

	-ar	camin***ar*** (to walk)
yo	**-o**	camin***o***
tú	**-as**	camin***as***
usted	**-a**	camin***a***
él/ella	**-a**	camin***a***
nosotros/as	**-amos**	camin***amos***
vosotros/as	**-áis**	camin***áis***
ustedes	**-an**	camin***an***
ellos/ellas	**-an**	camin***an***

-er Verbs, Present Tense

	-er	beber (to drink)
yo	-o	bebo
tú	-es	bebes
usted	-e	bebe
él/ella	-e	bebe
nosotros/as	-emos	bebemos
vosotros/as	- éis	bebéis
ustedes	-en	beben
ellos/ellas	-en	beben

-ir Verbs, Present Tense

	-ir	escribir (to write)
yo	-o	escribo

tú	-es	escribes
usted	-e	escribe
él/ella	-e	escribe
nosotros/as	-imos	escribimos
vosotros/as	- ís	escribís
ustedes	-en	escriben
ellos/ellas	-en	escriben

Stem Changing Verbs

These are verbs that conjugate with similar rules as the -ar, -er, and -ir examples above, but the stem (the first part of the word) shows an additional change. These changes are reflected in all conjugations except when nosotros or vosotros is used.

There are three common types of stem changes.

E becomes IE

	-er	querer (to want)
yo	-o	quiero
tú	-es	quieres
usted	-e	quiere
él/clla	-e	quiere
nosotros/as	-emos	queremos
vosotros/as	-éis	queréis
ustedes	-en	quieren
ellos/ellas	-en	quieren

Practice with these examples:

mentir (lie/fib), empezar (begin), pensar (think), perder (lose)

O becomes UE

	-ir	dormir (to sleep)
yo	-o	duermo
tú	-es	duermes
usted	-e	duerme
él/ella	-e	duerme
nosotros/as	-imos	dormimos
vosotros/as	- ís	dormís
ustedes	-en	duermen
ellos/ellas	-en	duermen

Practice with these examples:

volar (fly), morir (die), encontrar (find), doler (hurt)

E becomes I

-ir	Reír (to sleep)	
yo	-o	río
tú	-es	ries
usted	-e	ríe
él/ella	-e	ríe
nosotros/as	-imos	reimos
vosotros/as	- ís	reís
ustedes	-en	ríen
ellos/ellas	-en	ríen

Practice with these examples:

pedir (ask), servir (serve), medir (measure), seguir (follow)

Progressive Verbs

These are for actions that are currently in progress. This would be the equivalent of saying someone is reading, leaping, climbing, or skiing. These verbs in English end with an -ing, whereas Spanish progressive verbs have the following endings:

-ar verbs will end with an -ando

-er and -ir verbs will end with -iendo

Additionally, progressive verbs are used along with the word estar (to be), which is conjugated in the following manner.

Yo	estoy cocinando	I am cooking.
Tú	estás trabajando	You are working.
Usted	está diciendo	You are saying…
él/ella	está bailando	He/She is dancing.
nosotros/as	estamos saliendo	We are dating.
vosotros	estáis quejando	You are complaining.
ustedes	están apoyando	You are supporting.
ellos/ellas	están tramando	They are scheming.

Progressive verbs can also replace the word 'estar' with any of the following (See the irregular verbs section below to see a few more relevant conjugations):

Andar – In the process of doing something.

> Ellas andan rescatando al principe.
>
> They are rescuing the prince.

Ir – To gradually begin something.

Ustedes van comprendiendo el drama.

You are starting to understand the drama.

Llevar – Have been doing something.

Tu llevas dos horas en el teléfono.

You have been on the phone for two hours.

Seguir – To continue doing something.

Ellas siguen ganando la competencia.

They keep winning the competition.

Venir – Have been doing something.

Él venía exlicando esto desde esta mañana.

He has been explaining this since this morning.

Irregular Verbs

Given all the scenarios above, there are still words that play by their own rules. As these words are very common, they are worth learning.

Irregular Yo

These are words that mostly follow the rules, but they deviate only in the me (yo) conjugations. One common change is with verbs that end with -guir, -ger, or -gir. In these scenarios, -guir becomes -go, and -ger/-gir becomes -jo.

Extinguir (to extinguish) yo extingo

Recoger (to pick up)	yo recojo
Dirigir (to direct)	yo dirijo

Other words simply have yo forms that go different directions all their own. Here are some examples.

Caber (to fit)	yo quepo
Saber (to know)	yo sé
Conozer (to know)	yo conozco
Dar (to give)	yo doy
Valer (to be worth)	yo valgo
Traer (to bring)	yo traigo
Caer (to fall)	yo caigo
Ver (to see)	yo veo
Poner (to put)	yo pongo
Traducer (to translate)	yo traduzco

Irregular in All Forms

There are words that do not follow any of the common conjugations in any of the forms. Here are four of them.

	ser	estar	ir	haber
	(to be)	(to be)	(to go)	(to have)
Yo	soy	estoy	voy	he
Tú	eres	estás	vas	has
Usted	es	está	va	ha, hay
él/ella	es	está	va	ha, hay
nosotros/as	somos	estamos	vamos	hemos
vosotros	sois	estáis	vais	habéis
ustedes	son	están	van	han

ellos/ellas	son	están	van	han

Conjugating Past Tense

	-ar	-er or -ir
yo	-é	-í
tú	-aste	-iste
usted	-ó	-ió
él/ella	-ó	-ió
nosotros/as	-amos	-imos
vosotros/as	-asteis	-isteis
ustedes	-aron	-ieron
ellos/ellas	-aron	-ieron

Recall that exceptions exist for irregular verbs. Here are a few examples to show these conjugations are in use:

buscar (to search)

busque, buscaste, buscó, buscasteis, buscaron.

esconder (to hide)

escondí, escondiste, escondío, escondimos, escondieron

conducir (to drive)

conduje, conduciste, conducío, conducimos, conducieron

descansar (to rest)

descanse, descansaste, descansó, descansteis, descansaron

Conjugating Future Tense

This is by far the easiest tense to conjugate. The suffixes -ar, -er, and -ir are all treated the same here. On top of that, nothing is dropped. Simply add the proper ending from the list below:

yo	-é
tú	-ás
usted	-á
él/ella	-á
nosotros/as	-emos
vosotros/as	-éis
ustedes	-án
ellos/ellas	-án

Here are a few examples. Keep an eye out for an irregular conjugation.

cantar (to sing)

cantaré, cantarás , cantará , cantaremos, cantaréis

venir (to come)

vendré, vendrás, vendrá, vendremos, vendréis, vendrán

pintar (to paint)

pintaré, pintarás, pintará, pintaremos, pintaréis

aprender (to learn)

aprenderé, aprenderás, aprenderá, aprenderemos

Conjugating Consecutive Verbs

At times you will see a pair of verbs that are referring to the same subject making a single action. A pattern you will notice with such pairing is that you do not conjugate both verbs, even though the tense and person taking the action are the exact same. One of these verbs is referred to as the "spine" verb, usually the first one. When it comes to conjugating these situations, you only need to work on this spine verb. The remaining word stays in the indefinite, unconjugated form (ending in -ir, -ar, -er). Exceptions exist to this, but you will see this in practice in most scenarios.

I hope to swim again	Yo espero nadar de nuevo
They will hope to swim	Ellos esperarán nadar
We have hoped to swim	Hemos esperado nadar

Careful with this rule though. You might be tempted to assume you are working with a spine verb situation when verbs get too close. However, as the example below shows, sometime an extra subject or noun slips in and creates the need to conjugate each verb.

I hope we swim	Espero que nadamos

Common Greetings

Hello	Hola
Good Morning	Buenos Días
Good Evening	Buenas Tardes
Good Night	Buenas Noches
Goodbye	Adiós
Have a Good Day	Que Tenga Usted Buenos Días
It is Nice to See You	Que Gusto de Verte
How have you been?	¿Cómo has estado?

Long Time No See — Tanto Tiempo sin Verte

Definite Articles

Where the English language might have a gotten away with a catch all word like "the", the Spanish language has 4 words in its place: El, La, Los, Las.

- **The** boy went to **the** store.
  El niño fue a **la** tienda.

- **The** girls have passed **the** exams.
  Las niñas han pasado **los** exámenes.

The Spanish language places a gender on every single noun, labeling them either as masculine or feminine.

Most nouns that refer to a living being will have two versions: One that (usually) ends in an -o for masculine, and another that ends in an -a for feminine.

The professor	el profesor, la profesora
The American	el americano, la americana
The scientist	el científico, la científica

Gender is also applied to all nouns, including inanimate objects. Learning which words are masculine and which words are feminine will mostly come with practice, but the following guide should help you get started:

Words that end in -ma, -pa, or the letters L, O, N, E, R, S are usually masculine, but exceptions exist all the time.

Words that end in -ión, -dad, -tad, -tud, and the letter A are mostly feminine, with exceptions.

Nouns are also singular or plural in the same way you see them in the English language.

The Spanish language uses 'El, La, Los, Las' in the following manner:

The knife	El cuchillo (Singular masculine)
The burger	La hamburguesa (Singular feminine)
The plates	Los platos (Plural masculine)
The chairs	Las sillas (Plural feminine)

An exception is made for situations where you would end up with repeating 'a' sounds next to each other. However, once you have an adjective that removes the repeating 'a' sound, the exception no longer exists.

The eagle	El águila (feminine)
The same eagle	La misma águila (feminine)

Animals
Animales

Mouse	El ratón
Bird	El pájaro
Cat	El gato
Dog	El perro
Rabbit	El conejo
Elephant	El elefante
Lizard	el lagarto
Squirrel	la ardilla
Rhino	el rinoceronte
Pig	el cerdo
Cow	la vaca
Chicken	el pollo

Turkey	El pavo
Peacock	el pavo real

Interrogatives

These common questions exist in both English and Spanish, but one major change exists in the punctuation. The beginning of the interrogation is marked by an upside-down question mark.

Who? ¿Quién?

- ¿Quién soltó los perros?
  Who let the dogs out?

What? ¿Qué?

- ¿Qué debo traer para la caminata de mañana?
  What should I bring for tomorrow's hike?

Where? ¿Dónde?

- ¿Dónde compraste esa camisa genial?
  Where did you buy that cool shirt?

When? ¿Cuándo?

- ¿Cuándo es la próxima reunión del equipo?
  When is the next team meeting?

Why? ¿Por qué?

- ¿Por qué están abiertas las ventanas?
  Why are the windows open?

How? ¿Cómo?

- ¿Cómo encontraste mi escondite de dulces?
  How did you find my candy stash?

It is important to know some key words to responding to these kinds of questions. Useful terms are as follows:

Yes	Sí
No	No
I do not know	No sé
I have no idea	No tengo ni idea
Because	Porque
Of course	Por supuesto

Numbers
Números

Zero	Cero
One	Uno
Two	Dos
Three	Tres
Four	Cuatro
Five	Cinco
Six	Seis
Seven	Siete
Eight	Ocho
Nine	Nueve
Ten	Diez
Eleven	Once
Twelve	Doce
Thirteen	Trece
Fourteen	Catorce
Fifteen	Quince

Sixteen	Dieciséis
Seventeen	Diecisiete
Eighteen	Dieciocho
Nineteen	Diecinueve
Twenty	Veinte

Did you notice a pattern starting to form after 15? Those numbers begin to follow the format of "ten and six, ten and seven…" as a single word. The pattern continues through the twenties. Veinteuno, veintedós, veintetrés…

Thirty	Treinta

At this point, the number is now broken into seperate words, but the pattern is the same. Treinta y uno, treinta y dos…

Forty	Cuarenta
Fifty	Cincuenta
Sixty	Sesenta
Seventy	Setenta
Eighty	Ochenta
Ninety	Noventa
Hundred	Cien

Numbers after this continue the pattern without the 'y'. Ciento uno, ciento dos…

Two Hundred	Doscientos
Three Hundred	Trescientos
Four Hundred	Cuatroscientos
Five Hundred	Quinientos
Six Hundred	Seiscientos
Seven Hundred	Setecientos

Eight Hundred	Ochocientos
Nine Hundred	Novecientos
Thousand	Mil

Now you have the tools to describe numbers well beyond a thousand, which can be rather useful when you want to read the important dates out of any history book.

Ordinable Numbers

First	Primero
Second	Segundo
Third	Tercera
Fourth	Cuatro
Fifth	Quinto
Sixth	Sexto
Seventh	Séptimo
Eighth	Octavo
Ninth	Noveno
Tenth	Décimo
Eleventh	Undécimo
Twelfth	Duodécimo
Thirteenth	Decimotercero
Fourteenth	Decimocuarto
Fifteenth	Decimoquinto
Sixteenth	Decimosexto
Seventeenth	Decimoséptimo
Eighteenth	Decimoctavo
Nineteenth	Decimonoveno

Twentieth	Vigésimo
Twenty First	Vigésimo primero
Twenty Second	Vigesimo segundo
Thirtieth	Trigésimo
Thirty First	Trigésimo primero
Fourtieth	Cuadragésimo
Fiftieth	Quincuagésimo
Sixtieth	Sexagésimo
Seventieth	Septuagésimo
Eightieth	Octogésimo
Ninetieth	Nonagésimo
Hundreth	Centreth
Thousandth	Milésimo

Conjunctions

The Spanish language does not favor repeating vowel sounds. That is to say that when you are listing items and you have a word that begins with the same sound as the conjunction, you will use the alternate version.

You will see this with words like 'y' and 'o'.

And — y (sometimes e)

- Las clases serán los lunes y martes.
  Classes will be on Mondays and Tuesdays.

- Me motivas e inspiras para ser una mejor artista.
  You motivate and inspire me to be a better artist.

Either… Or — O… O (sometime u)

- O son gemelos, o estoy viendo doble.
  Either you are twins, or I am seeing double.

- Creo que cumple diez u once años.
  I believe he turns ten or eleven years old.

Neither… Nor Ni… Ni

- Ni Jorge ni Rebecca sabía en cual autobús debían viajar.
- Neither Jorge nor Rebecca knew which bus they needed to be on.

That is to say Es Decir

- No tengo jugo. Es decir, solo puedo ofrecerte agua.
  I don't have any juice. That is to say I can only offer you water.

Even Though Aunque, A pesar de que

- Gané el segundo lugar a pesar de que tropecé.
  I won second place even though I tripped.

But/yet Pero/mas

- Me quedé despierto para estudiar, pero la prueba es la semana siguiente.
  I stayed up to study, but the test is the following week.

Instead En cambio

- En cambio, pediré un té, ya que no hay café.
  I'll order tea instead, since there's no coffee.

However Sin Embargo

- Sin embargo, ocuparé su lugar en la competencia.
  However, I will take her place in the competition.

If Si

- Si preparas la cena, puedo limpiar este desastre.
  If you make dinner, I can clean this mess.

Colors
Colores

Red	Rojo
Pink	Rosa
Blue	Azul
Green	Verde
Yellow	Amarillo
Purple	Morado
Orange	Naranja
Brown	Café
Black	Negro
Gray	Gris
White	Blanco

Parts of the Body
Partes del Cuerpo

Nose	La nariz
Ears	Las orejas
Mouth	La boca
Head	La cabeza
Stomach	El estómago
Hands	Las manos
Feet	Los pies
Heart	Corazón
Liver	Hígado
Kidneys	Riñones
Bones	Huesos

Muscles	Músculos
Tendons	Tendones
Joints	Articulaciones
Shoulders	Espalda
Knees	Rodillas
Elbows	Codos
Chest	Pecho
Fingers	Dedos
Toes	Dedos de los pies

Home

Family Members

Miembros de la Familia

Father, Dad	El padre, El papá
Mother, Mom	La madre, La mamá
Brother	El hermano
Sister	La hermana
Uncle	El tío
Aunt	La tía
Grandfather	El abuelo
Grandmother	La abuela
Son	El hijo
Daughter	La hija
Nephew	El sobrino
Niece	La sobrina
Neighbor	El vecino
Friend	El amigo

Pronouns

Him / Her	Él / Élla
His / Hers	Suyo / Suya
Them	Éllos, Éllas
Theirs	Su, Suyo
You (informal, friendly)	Tú
You (formal, respectful)	Usted

Me	Yo

Cognates and False Cognates

You may have noticed that a large number of words look similar between the two languages. When they happen to have the same meaning, they are called cognates. Sometimes the words are spelled the same and you can recognize them when you hear them, even though they might be pronounced differently.

Chocolate	el chocolate
Violin	el violín
Confusion	la confusión
Musical	el musical

Some words look like they almost match, with some small changes.

Action	la acción
Salary	el salario
Organic	orgánico
Basic	Lo básico

This can be a comfort as you encounter new words since you practically know some of them already. As you learn to speak more comfortably in Spanish, you will find yourself in situations where you have an idea to convey, but you are struggling to think of the right word in Spanish. You might even feel confident enough to take a guess, especially if you are pretty sure you heard someone use that word before.

Consider the situation where you accidentally dropped a dish and you are trying to apologize in Spanish. You want to say you are embarrassed by the situation, and you want to clean up the mess. You take a guess and end up saying –Lo siento mucho, estoy embarazado. Yo voy a limpiar esto.

Suddenly you hear another dish drop. Someone in the back yells out – ¡¿Que?!

You are now surrounded by people that are either congratulating or demanding answers from you. What happened?

Well, it turns out you forgot to review the emotions section of this book. Instead of admitting you were embarrassed, you just told everyone that you were pregnant.

- Lo siento mucho, estoy **avergonzado**. Yo voy a limpiar esto.
  I am very sorry. I am embarrassed. I will clean up the mess.

La fabrica	Factory (Not fabric)
La carpeta	Binder, folder (Not carpet)
La decepcion	Let down, disappointment (Not deception)
La tuna	Prickly pear (Not tuna fish)
Enviar	to send (Not envy)
Recordar	to remember (Not to record)

Word Order in Sentences

The placement of adjectives and nouns in a sentence is different between English and Spanish.

In Spanish, adjectives will go after the noun, not before. This means the phrase 'the broken pencil' in English will then become 'the pencil broken' in Spanish.

Notice how the order of words switches:

- The broken pencil
  El lapiz roto

- The small red bird
  El pajarito rojo

- The soft gray fur
  El pelaje gris y suave

. The English language has several rules regarding the priority of adjectives for situations when several are used on a single noun. The Spanish language does not have such a rigid structure. The sentence can sound a bit jumbled if you use more than a couple, but you are free to experiment with the order.

Prepositions

This	Este
That	Ese
Here	Aquí
There	Allí
Left	Izquierda
Right	Derecha
Ahead of	Adelante de
Behind	Detrás de
Above	Sobre
Below	Debajo

Rooms of the House

Habitaciones de la Casa

Kitchen	La cocina
Living Room	La sala
Dining Room	El comedor
Bedroom	El dormitorio
Bathroom	El baño

Household Chores

Quehaceres Domésticos

Vacuuming the carpet	Aspirando la alfombra
Wiping the counter	Limpiando la encimera
Washing the dishes	Lavando los platos
Organizing laundry	Organizar la ropa
Throwing out the trash	Tirar la basura
Washing the truck	Lavando el camion

Emotions

Happy	Contento, Feliz
Sad	Triste
Relaxed	Relajado
Angry	Enfadado
Bored	Aburrido
Scared	Asustado
Tired	Cansado
In Love	Enamorado
Embarrassed	Avergonzado

Technology

Phone	El teléfono
Headphones	los audífonos
Television	La televisión
Computer	La computadora
Laptop	El portatil

Tablet	La tableta
Charger	El cargador
Adaptor	El adaptor

Events

Expressing Time
Expresando el Tiempo

Seconds	Los segundos
Minutes	Los minutos
Hours	Las horas
Days	Los dias
Now	Ahora
Then	Entonces
Before	Antes
After	Después
During	Durante
Since	Desde
By, until	Hasta
Hours ago	hace unas horas
AM	de la mañana
PM	de la Tarde
Today	Hoy
Tomorrow	Mañana
Yesterday	Ayer

Day Before Yesterday	Antier
After Tomorrow	Pasado Mañana
This Week	Esta Semana
Next Week	La Próxima Semana
This Month	Este Mes
Last Month	El Mes Pasado

Days of the Week
Días de la Semana

Monday	Lunes
Tuesday	Martes
Wednesday	Miércoles
Thursday	Jueves
Friday	Viernes
Saturday	Sábado
Sunday	Domingo

Months of the Year
Meses del Año

January	Enero
February	Febrero
March	Marzo
April	Abril
May	Mayo
June	Junio

July	Julio
August	Agosto
September	Septiembre
October	Octubre
November	Noviembre
December	Diciembre

Seasons and Holidays

Happy holidays	Felices vacaciones
Happy Birthday	Feliz cumpleaños
How old are you?	¿Cuantos años tienes?
Happy New Year	Feliz año nuevo
Merry Christmas	Feliz Navidad
Seasons	Estaciones
Spring	La primavera
Summer	El verano
Autumn	El otoño
Winter	El invierno

Shopping

Buying Clothing and Accessories

Comprando ropa y accesorios

Socks	Los calcetines
Pants	Los pantalones
Shirt	La camisa

Undershirt	La camiseta
Underwear	Los calzones
Boxers	Los boxers
Panties	Las bragas
Briefs	Los calzoncillos
Belt	El cinturon
Shoes	Los zapatos
Boots	Las botas
Hat	El sombrero

Method of Payment
Forma de pago

Money	El dinero
Cash	El dinero en efectivo
Cash or credit?	¿Efectivo o crédito?
Credit card	Tarjeta de crédito
Debit	Débito
Writing a check	Escribir un cheque
Making a transaction	Realizas un Transacción
Payment plans	Planes de pago
Taking out a loan	Sacar un préstamo
I pay all of my debts	Pago todas mis deudas
Staying out of debt	Manenerse libre de deudas

School and Office
Escuela y Oficina

School supplies	Los útiles escolares
Office Supplies	Los suministros de oficina
Back to school sale	Venta de regreso a las escuela
Computer	La computadora
Backpack	La mochila
Pencil	El lápiz
Pen	El bolígrafo, El plumon
Markers	Los marcadores
Eraser	El borrador
Pencil lead	La mina del lápiz
Mechanical pencil	El portaminas
Book	El libro
Printer paper	El papel de la impresora
Copy machine	La fotocopiadora
Fax machine	La maquina de fax
Coffee pot	La cafetería
Voicemail	Mensaje de voz

Dining

Common Courtesies

Thank you	Gracias
You're welcome	De nada

No problem	No hay problema
It was my pleasure	Era mi placer
Excuse me	Disculpe
I am sorry	Lo Siento
Good luck	Buena suerte
Take care	Cuídate
Get well soon	Mejorate Pronto
Bless you	Salud

The Five Senses
Los Cinco Sentidos

See	Ver
Hear	Oír
Listen	Escuchar
Smell	Oler
Touch	Tocar
Taste	Probar
What is that smell?	¿Que es ese olor?
What do you see?	¿Que ves?
This tastes great.	Esto sabe muy bien
This tastes terrible.	Esto sabe terrible
That smells delicious.	Huele delicioso
I am cold.	Tengo frío
It is hot in here.	Hace calor
What is that sound?	¿Qué es ese sonido?

I cannot hear anything. No puedo escuchar nada

Rules for Accents and When to Use Them

Accents were explained briefly in the first section of this book. At this point we will cover the details on them with greater detail. Accents indicate to a reader that the marked syllable is stressed, or which syllable carries an emphasis when the word is pronounced.

The stressing of syllables occurs the same way between English and Spanish. Only one syllable can be stressed, and every word has a stressed syllable. These are easy to forget about in English as they are not marked.

Regardless, they make the difference between heading towards the **<u>en</u>**trance of a jewelry store, or simply letting the display en**<u>trance</u>** you without you entering at all.

The use of accent marks, called tildes, lets the reader immediately which pronunciation is appropriate.

You likely have wondered about how one pronounces words that do not have accent marks. Simply need to look at the last letter in the word and follow one of these two rules:

1. If the word ends in a vowel, n, or s, then the stress is on the next-to-last syllable.

   <u>Ca</u>lle (street), **<u>tiem</u>**po (time), **<u>li</u>**bros (books)
   Biblio**<u>te</u>**ca (library), a**<u>den</u>**tro (inside)

2. If the word ends in a consonant, except for n or s, then the stress is on the last syllable.

   Pa**<u>pel</u>** (paper), re**<u>loj</u>** (clock), tam**<u>bor</u>** (drum)
   Cara**<u>col</u>** (snail)

Any situation that does not follow either of these rules will always have an accent mark.

Compré (bought), inglés (english), balcón (balcony)

árbol (tree), azúcar (sugar), túnel (tunnel)

América (America), pájaro (bird), teléfono (telephone)

Científicamente (scientifically), gánatela (earn it)

If you want to have a better grasp on these rules, review all the vocabulary in this book. When you see a word without an accent, use these rules to help you decide which syllable is stressed. Otherwise get in the habit of emphasizing the stressed syllable. Doing this will help you sound more fluent in Spanish.

What do you do if you know how to pronounce a word, but you need to write the accent symbol in yourself? The process is the same, only backwards. Figure out which syllable is stressed and based on that you figure out which rule applies.

If the last syllable is stressed, you will only add a tilde if the last letter is vowel, n, or s.

If the second to last syllable is stressed, you will only add a tilde if the last letter is a consonant, except for n or s.

If the third to last or the fourth to last syllable is stressed, this will always need to have the accent marked.

If you are presented with a very large word, focus on the last four syllables. Stressed syllables do not really go further back than that.

Review the last set of example words that have their stressed syllables in bold. These examples are in order from stress on the last syllable, to stress on the fourth to last. These rules are seen in these same examples.

Accents to Differentiate Words

You must also be aware that these rules regarding accents are not all there is to consider. In the same way that English is filled with homophones and homographs, you will see there are words that different Spanish words look very similar, but they have very different meaning. Earlier you saw the impact of using the letter H to create a distinction between words like ola (ocean wave) and hola (hello). Here we will focus on words that have the exact same letters, but an accent is used to mark their distinction.

papá	Father
papa	Potato
te	Conjugation of you (te amo – I love you)
té	Tea
cual	"That" – Relative person or thing.
	El hombre cual me ayudo…
	The man that helped me…
cuál	"Which" or "What" – Interrogative
	¿Cuál es el matón?
	Which one is the bully?
como	"as" or "like" Conjunction
	Como te dije antes...
	Like I told you before…
cómo	How? – Exclamatory or Interrogative
	¿Cómo pasó esto?
	How did this happen?
este	This – Adjective, or the Eastern direction
	Este pan se echó a perder.
	This bread went bad.
éste	This one – Pronoun
	Éste baila como un tonto.
	This one dances like a fool.
aquel	That – Adjective
	Aquel sujeto que vino ayer.
	That guy who came yesterday.

aquél	That one – Pronoun
	Aquél es el sujeto. – That is the guy.
cuanto	How much – Adjective or adverb
	Cuanto más me grites, menos te escucharé
	The more you yell at me, the less I will listen.
cuánto	How much? – Interrogative
	¿Cuántas monedas me debes?
	How many coins do you owe me?
donde	Where – Adjective or adverb
	Donde todas las cosas son iguales.
	Where all things are equal.
dónde	Where? – Interrogative
	¿Dónde están todas las cosas?
	Where are all the things?
quien	Who – adjective or adverb
	Fue ella quien sonó al timbre.
	It was she who rang the doorbell.
quién	Who? – Interrogative
	¿Quien está en la puerta?
	Who is at the door?

Groceries

Apples	Las manzanas
Oranges	Las naranjas
Bananas	Los plátanos
Bread	El pan

Cookies	Las galletas
Vegetables	Los verduras
Fruit	La fruta
Meat	La carne
Butter	La mantequilla
Flour	La harina
Onion	La cebolla
Garlic	El ajo
Salt	La sal
Coffee	El café
Tea	El té
Soda	La soda
Water	El agua
Beans	Los frijoles
Rice	El arroz
Soup	La sopa
Tortillas	Las tortillas
Salsa	La salsa
Peppers	Los pimientos
Bell peppers	Los pimientos morrones
Black peppers	La pimienta negra
Jalapeno	Jalapeño

Placing an Order at the Restaurant

- Where is the waiter?

¿Dónde está el camarero?

- I am ready to order.
  Estoy listo para ordenar.

- What are my options for drinks?
  ¿Cuáles son mis opciones de bebidas?

- What do you recommend?
  ¿Que recomiendas?

- I will have the special.
  Tendré el especial.

- I would like more.
  Quisiera mas

- No more, please.
  No mas por favor.

- This is not what I ordered.
  Esto no es lo que pedí.

Common Food Allergies

Cow's Milk	Leche de Vaca
Eggs	Los huevos
Tree Nuts	Los nueces
Peanuts	Los cacahuates
Shellfish	Los mariscos
Wheat	El trigo
Soy	La soja
Fish	El pescado

Breakfast
El desayuno

Soft boiled eggs	Los huevos pasados por agua
Hard boiled eggs	Los huevos duros
Poached eggs	Los huevos escalfados
Sunny side up	Con las yemas boca arriba
Eggs over easy	Los huevos estrellados
Fried eggs	Los huevos fritos
Scrambled eggs	Los huevos revueltos
Bacon	El tocino
Hash browns	Los hash browns
Toast	La tostada
Muffins	Los muffins
Pancakes	Los panqueques
Waffles	Los gofres

Traveling

Places of Interest and Common Hobbies

Mall	El centro comercial
Restaurant	El restaurante
Library	La biblioteca
Book Store	La librería
Office	La oficina
Post Office	Oficina de Correos
Movie Theater	El cine
Zoo	El zoológico

Hotel	El hotel
Hospital	El hospital
School	La escuela
Work	El trabajo

Travel Options

Car	El auto
Truck	El camión
Train	El tren
Station	El estación
Airplane	El avión
Airport	El aeropuerto
Bicycle	La bicicleta
Taxi	El taxi

Giving and Getting Directions

North — Norte

East — Este

South — Sur

West — Oeste

Down the road. — Por el camino.

Turn left at the stop sign.

Gire a la izquierda en la senal de pare.

Third building on the right.

Tercer edificio a la derecha.

A few streets later.

Unas calles mas tarde.

Turn after the big rock, you cannot miss it.

Gira despues de la roca grande, no se la puede perder.

Idioms

Translating between English and Spanish can be tricky, in part because a literal word for word translation is not accurate. We see this in simple word order situations (the balloon red vs the red balloon), but it is far more drastic when you look at figures of speech or colloquialisms.

When you say a cat has got your tongue, we do not literally mean a stray cat came by and ran off with a piece of your actual tongue. Yet we understand the meaning because we hear the phrase used often enough.

To translate something like this, you must translate the meaning instead. "You have been unusually quiet" becomes "Has estado inusualmente tranquila"

There are several phrases that similarly do not translate literally from Spanish to English.

Estar en la edad del pavo.

Literally: To be in the age of the turkey.

Meaning: To be a teenager.

Estar como una cabra.

Literally: To be like a goat.

Meaning: To be crazy.

No ver tres en un burro.

Literally: Not being able to see three on a donkey.

Meaning: Having bad vision.

Verle las orejas al lobo/

Literally: To see the ears of the wolf.

Meaning: To notice danger.

Dar gato por un liebre.

Literally: To give a cat for a hare.

Meaning:To trick or rip someone off.

Ser un melon.

Literally: To be a melon.

Meaning: To not be very intelligent.

Ponerse como un tomate.

Literally: To turn into a tomato.

Meaning: To blush.

No tener ni pies ni cabeza.

Literally: Without feet or a head.

Meaning: Not making any sense.

Sin pelos en la lengua.

Literally: Without hair on your tongue.

Meaning: To be outspoken.

Estar hasta las narices.

Literally: To be up to the nose.

Meaning: To be annoyed or tired of something.

Encontrar tu media naranja.

Literally: To find your half orange.

Meaning: To find the perfect partner.

Section 2: Stories for Beginners

1 - Ayúdame a Buscar a Mi Amigo.

–Estoy buscando a mi amigo Enrique. ¿Lo has visto?

–Yo no conozco Enrique, pero puedo ayudarte a buscarlo. ¿El como se parece?

–Bueno, sé que hoy llevaba su chaqueta verde.

–¡Oh! El Sr. Elefante llevaba una chaqueta verde. ¿Es este tu amigo?

–No, mi amigo es mucho más pequeño que eso. Enrique tiene orejas grandes.

–Señor. El conejo tiene orejas grandes, pero no he visto lo que llevaba puesto hoy.

–Yo conosco al Sr. Conejo, pero el todavía es demasiado alto.

–¿Tu amigo es aun más pequeño que él? ¿Cuál es su apellido?

–El también es conocido como el Sr. Ratón.

–Señor Raton era mi padre. Puedes llamarme Enrique.

–¡Ahí tienes! ¡Te estaba buscando por todas partes!

Help Me Look for My Friend.

"I am looking for my friend, Enrique. Have you seen him?"

"I do not know an Enrique, but I can help you look for him. What does he look like?"

"Well, I know he was wearing his green jacket today."

"Oh! Mr. Elephant was wearing a green jacket. Is this your friend?"

"No, my friend is much shorter than that. Enrique does have large ears though."

"Mr. Rabbit has large ears, but I have not seen what he was wearing today."

"I have met Mr. Rabbit, but he is still too tall."

"Your friend is even shorter than him? What is his last name?"

"He is also known as Mr. Mouse."

"Mr. Mouse was my father. You can just call me Enrique."

"There you are! I was looking all over for you!"

2 – Cortando Cebollas

–¿Estás llorando? ¿Qué está mal?

–Nada. Estoy preparando la cena. Siempre lloro cuando corto cebollas.

–Oh, mi error. Pensé que estabas triste. ¿Qué estás cocinando?

–Arroz.

–¿Arroz? ¿Se utilizan cebollas para hacer arroz?

–Solo si quieres que sepa bien.

–¡Bueno! Te daré espacio para cocinar en paz.

–Gracias.

–Espera un minuto, ¿por que hay un libro en el estante para platos?

–¿Qué? ¿Quién puso eso ahí?

–¿Lo estabas leyendo hace un momento?

–No seas tonto, estoy cocinando arroz.

–Por supuesto. ¿Pero dónde están las cebollas?

Cutting Onions

"Are you crying? What is wrong?"

"Nothing. I am preparing dinner. I always cry when I cut onions."

"Oh, my mistake. I thought you were sad. What are you making?"

"Rice."

"Rice? Are onions used to make rice?"

"They are if you want it to taste good."

"Good to know! I will give you space to cook in peace."

"Thank you."

"Wait a minute, is that a book in the dish rack?"

"What? Who put that there?"

"Were you reading it just now?"

"Do not be silly, I am cooking rice."

"Of course. But where are the onions?"

3 – Asistencia de Compras

Pablo fue a la tienda de ropa porque necesitaba una chaqueta nueva. Su chaqueta vieja tenía agujeros y necesitaba algo nuevo para ponerse que fuera cómodo. Su vieja chaqueta era verde, pero el vio una chaqueta roja que le gustó. Se lo probó, pero no le resultó cómodo. De hecho, ninguna de las otras chaquetas le quedaba bien. Una joven que trabajaba allí se le acercó y le preguntó si necesitaba ayuda. El explicó que quería comprar una chaqueta nueva, pero nada le quedaba.

–¿Señor? ¿Esta chaqueta es para ti o para una amiga?

–Es para mi.

–Bueno, esta es la sección de mujeres. ¿Quieres que te muestre dónde está la sección de hombres?"

Shopping Assistance

Pablo went to the clothing store because he needed a new jacket, His old jacket had holes in it, and he needed something new to wear that was comfortable. His old jacket was green, but he saw a red jacket that he liked. He tried it on, but it was not comfortable. In fact, none of the other jackets fit him. A young woman that worked there approached him and asked if he needed any help. He explained that he wanted to buy a new jacket, but nothing fit him.

"Sir? Is this jacket for you or for a friend?"

"It is for me."

"Well, this is the woman's section. Would you like me to show you where the men's section is?"

4 – Un Nuevo Amigo

Veronica acababa de mudarse de un apartamento a una casa. Estaba muy emocionada porque finalmente pudo conseguir un perro. Se había asegurado de que la nueva casa tuviera un jardín solo para su perro. Primero, fue a la tienda y le compró todo lo que necesitaba. Luego fue al refugio para encontrar el perro perfecto.

Había perros grandes, perros pequeños y de todos los tamaños intermedios. Había diferentes colores, con diferentes cantidades de cabello. Algunos perros eran viejos y otros jóvenes. Ella había querido un cachorro, pero cada cachorro era demasiado ruidoso y enérgico para ella. Comenzó a mirar a los perros mayores y vio uno que tenía ocho años, un ojo, cinco dientes y la nariz roja. Era el perro más lindo que había visto en su vida.

–¡Discúlpeme señor! – Ella preguntó. –¿Puedo tener este perro?

A New Friend

Veronica had just moved from an apartment to a house. She was very excited because she could finally get a dog. She had made sure the new house had a garden just for her dog. First, she went to the store and bought him everything he would need. She then went to the shelter to find the perfect dog. There were big dogs, small dogs, and every size in between. There were different colors, with different lengths of hair. Some dogs were old, and some were young. She had wanted a puppy, but each puppy was too loud and too energetic for her. She started to look at the older dogs and saw one that was eight years old and had one eye, five teeth, and a red nose. He was the cutest dog she had ever seen.

"Excuse me sir!" She asked. May I have this dog?

5 – Oficina de Correos

Rebecca fue a la oficina de correos porque necesitaba enviarle una tarjeta de cumpleaños a su tía.

Su tía vivía cientos de millas en distancia, y Rebecca quería asegurarse de haber enviado la carta este día. Ella llegó al mostrador y encontro un simpático anciano que se ofreció a ayudarla.

–Necesito enviarle esto a mi tía.

–Está bien", dijo el señor, y peso la tarjeta para ella. –Esto será un dólar para enviar.

Ella buscó su billetera pero no pudo encontrarla.

–¡Oh no! Olvidé mi billetera en la casa.

Afortunadamente, la señora detrás de ella ofreció a pagar.

–¡Muchísimas gracias! Este correo era urgente.

–No te preocupes por eso. Yo tambien he olvidado mi billetera antes.

Post Office

Rebecca went to the post office because she needed to send a birthday card to her aunt.

Her aunt lived hundreds of miles away, and Rebecca wanted to be sure she mailed the letter by today. She got to the counter and she saw a nice elderly man that offered to help.

"I need to mail this to my aunt."

"OK" he said, and he weighed the card for her. "This will be one dollar to mail."

She reached for her wallet but could not find it.

"Oh no! I forgot my wallet at home.

Luckily, the lady behind her offered to pay.

"Thank you very much! This mail was time sensitive."

"Do not worry about it. I have forgotten my wallet before."

6 – Reunión Familiar

Jaime nunca había conocido a su familia extendida, pero su mamá dijo que el tenía que ir a la reunión familiar. Cuando llegó, el reconoció a nadie. Su madre estaba tan feliz de ponerse al día con todos, lo dejó solo y corrió a ver a su hermana. Sin saber qué hacer, fue a buscar comida.

Cuando llegó allí, había unas ancianas que le sonreían.

–¿Hola, te conozco? –dijo el.

–Sí, somos tus tías abuelas. Nos conociste antes, cuando tenías cinco años.

–Pero ahora tengo veinte años, no te recuerdo en absoluto.

–Seguro que has visto fotos de nosotros.

–No…

–O escuché historias sobre nosotros.

–No…

Las tías abuelas se ofendieron mucho y fueron a buscar a su madre. Estaba solo de nuevo. Consiguió su comida, pero justo cuando estaba a punto de comer, un niño se le acercó. –¡Hola!

Jaime suspiró "Buenas tardes, ¿te conozco?

–No. No te preocupes, yo tampoco conozco a nadie aquí .

Family Reunion

Jaime had never met his extended family, but his mom said he had to go the family reunion. When he arrived, he did not recognize anybody. His mom was so happy to catch up with everybody, she left him alone and ran over to see her sister. Not knowing what to do, he went to go get food.

When he got there, there were some old ladies that were smiling at him.

"Hello, do I know you?"

"Yes, we are your great aunts. You have met us before, back when you were five."

"But I am twenty now, I do not remember you at all."

"Surely you have seen pictures of us."

"No…"

"Or heard stories about us."

"No…"

The great Aunts got very offended and went to look for his mother. He was alone again. He got his food, but just as he was about to eat, a young boy came up to him. "Hello!"

Jaime sighed "Good afternoon, do I know you?"

"No. Do not worry, I also do not know anybody here."

7 – Chispas

Rudolpho acababa de preparar el pastel perfecto, pero se dio cuenta de que no tenía chispas. Fue a la tienda de comestibles, pero no pudo encontrar chispas.

–Disculpe, –le preguntó a una señora que tenía una placa con su nombre –¿Sabes dónde están las chispas?

–Sí, estarán en el pasillo cuatro, a la derecha, en el segundo estante.

–¡Gracias! – él dijo.

Cuando llegó al pasillo cuatro, todo lo que vio fue refresco.

–¡Estos no son chispas! –Aún así miró a ambos lados del pasillo, pero no pudo encontrarlos. Le pidió ayuda a otro empleado.

–¡Oh! Tenemos esos pasillos quince. – Así que Rudolpho cruzó la tienda y todo lo que vio fueron velas. –¡No es lo que necesito!

Preguntó a otro empleado, y lo enviaron hasta el pasillo uno. Finalmente, encontró el lugar correcto. Sin embargo, todas se agotaron.

Sprinkles

Rudolpho had just made the perfect cake, but he realized he did not have any sprinkles. He went to the grocery store, but he could not find them.

"Excuse me" he asked a lady that had a name badge "do you know where the sprinkles are?"

"Yes, they will be on aisle four, on the right, on the second shelf."

"Thank you!" he said.

When he got to aisle four, all he saw was soda.

"These are not sprinkles!" He looked up and down the aisle but could not find them. He asked another employee for help.

"Oh! We have those aisle fifteen. So Rudolpho walked across the store and all he saw were candles. "The is not what I need!"

He asked another employee, and they sent him all the way to aisle one. Finally, he found the right place. However, they were all sold out.

8 – Prepararse

Archie tenía una entrevista de trabajo este lunes, así que necesitaba cortarse el pelo. Fue a la peluquería y se sentó en la silla.

–¿Qué tipo de corte de pelo quieres?

–Necesito algo agradable para una entrevista de trabajo.

–¡Excelente! No tengo idea de qué tipo de corte de pelo necesitas. ¿Quieres el pelo corto o largo? ¿Quizás te gustaría un poco de tinte para el cabello?

–Solo necesito un corte de pelo para una entrevista de trabajo.

–¿Quieres que tu cabello esté rizado? ¿Quieres probar este nuevo gel?

–No, solo quiero verme bien para la entrevista.

–Solo te daré un recorte.

–Eso está bien, solo haz que se vea bien.

Getting prepared

Archie had a job interview on Monday, so he needed to get a haircut. He went to barber shop and sat down at the chair.

"What kind of haircut do you want?"

"I need something nice for a job interview."

"Excellent! I have no idea what kind of haircut you need. Do you want the hair short or long? Perhaps you would like some hair dye?"

"I just need a haircut for a job interview."

"Do you want your hair curled. Do you want to try this new gel?"

"No, I just want to look good for the interview."

"I will just give you a trim them."

"That is fine, just make it look good."

9 – Levantando las Cajas

Pablo el pingüino necesitaba ayudar a su amigo a moverse.

Él estaba decidido a ser útil, pero sus aletas no tenían mucho agarre. Independientemente, tomó la caja más pesada que pudo y la subió por las escaleras. Sintió que se le resbalaba de las aletas, pero estaba a la mitad de las escaleras y no había nadie cerca para ayudarlo. Luchó, pero se las arregló para llevarlo hasta arriba sin ninguna ayuda. Él estaba tan emocionado cuando llegó a la cima, pero no vio la pequeña caja en su camino. Tropezó y dejó caer la caja grande.

Lifting Boxes

Pablo the penguin needed to help his friend move. He was determined to be useful, but his flippers did not have much grip. Regardless, he picked up the heaviest box he could and carried it up the stairs. He felt it slipping from his flippers, but he was halfway up the stairs, and no one was nearby to help. He struggled, but he managed to carry it all the way up without any help. He was so excited when he got to the top, but he did not see the small box in his path. He tripped and he dropped the big box.

10 – Un Mal Humor

El gato de Rosie se sentía mal, así que tuvo que meterlo en una caja y llevarlo al veterinario. Ella trató de hacer que la caja se sintiera cómoda, pero él estaba siseando y no quería que nadie lo tocara. Rosie trató de atraerlo con deliciosas golosinas y algunos de sus juguetes favoritos, pero él simplemente se metió debajo de la cama y gimió. Rosie incluso intentó usar un puntero láser, pero él no se movió. Frustrada, Rosie se arrastró debajo de la cama y lo agarró con tanto cuidado como pudo, pero se rascó. Cuando finalmente lo llevó al veterinario, ella advirtió al personal que estaba de mal humor. Pero cuando el personal abrió la caja, el gato de Rosie se mostró súper amigable. Sin embargo, el corte que ella recibió antes todavía le dolía.

A Bad Mood

Rosie's cat was feeling sick, so she had to put him in a crate and take him to the vet. She tried to make the crate comfortable, but he was hissing and did not want anyone to touch him. Rosie tried luring him in with tasty treats and some of his favorite toys, but he just went under the bed and groaned. Rosie even tried using a laser pointer, but he would not budge. Frustrates, Rosie crawled under the bed and grabbed him as carefully as she could, but she got scratched. When she finally got him to the vet, she warned the staff about him being in a bad mood. But when the staff opened the crate, Rosie's cat was super friendly. The cut she got earlier still hurt though.

11 – Un Viaje Divertido

Mi prima Cynthia tuvo un gran día en el zoológico. Me dijo que allí hay todo tipo de animales, desde pequeñas arañas y ratones hasta enormes elefantes y jirafas. Ella decía que los leones daban un poco de miedo, pero los tapires eran muy lindos. Le pregunté si los flamencos todavía estaban allí y dijo que eran su animal favorito que vio. Le gustaba el color rosa brillante que tenían las plumas y le gustaba imitar la forma en que se apoyaban en una sola pierna. Incluso me dijo que había un programa sobre insectos y le pusieron una tarántula en el hombro por un momento. Ella espera volver al zoológico algún día.

A Fun Trip

My cousin Cynthia had a great day at the zoo. She told me there are all sorts of animals there from tiny little spiders and mice to enormous elephants and giraffes. She said the lions were a little scary, but the tapirs were very cute. I asked her if the flamingos were still there, and she said they were her favorite animal she saw. She liked how bright pink the feathers were, and she liked to imitate the way they stood on one leg. She even told me there was a show about bugs and they put a tarantula on her shoulder for a moment. She looks forward to going back to the zoo someday.

12 – Alimentos Que No Puedo Comer

Franklin fue a la cafetería a la hora del almuerzo. Tenía hambre, pero la escuela no sabía que era alérgico al cacahuate. La escuela había preparado un almuerzo especial, ¡pero había cacahuetes por todas partes! El almuerzo de hoy fue sándwiches de manteca de cacahuate y mermelada, galletas de manteca de cacahuate, e incluso los batidos tenían sabor a manteca de cacahuate. Franklin estaba triste, no sabía lo que iba a hacer.

La señora de la cafetería hizo una lista de nombres, incluido Franklin, y pidió que cada uno de ellos viniera. Ella explicó que sabía sobre la alergia y que tenía una porción especial de pizza y leche con chocolate esperándolos. ¡Estaba delicioso!

Food That I Cannot Eat

Franklin went to the cafeteria for lunch time. He was hungry, but the school did not know he was allergic to peanuts. The school had made a special meal, but it had peanuts everywhere! Lunch today was peanut butter and jelly sandwiches, peanut butter cookies, and even the milkshakes were peanut butter flavored. Franklin was sad, he did not know what he was going to do.

The cafeteria lady called a list of names, including Franklin, and asked for each of them to come over. She explained that she knew about the allergy and had a special serving of pizza and chocolate milk waiting for them. It was delicious!

13 – ¡Largase!

Connie, el caballo, se iba de viaje de campamento con su familia. Esta era la primera vez que salía y no le gustaban los insectos. En la primera noche, hubo muchos insectos, incluso junto a la fogata. No le gustaban porque odiaba la sensación de que la mordieran. Ella trató de alejarse de ellos y se metió en la carpa, ¡pero ellos también estaban allí! Su madre le pidió que saliera de la carpa, tenía un repelente en aerosol para mantener alejados a los insectos. Connie salió y su madre le aplicó el repelente en el pelaje. Los bichos ya no la molestaban y Connie empezó a disfrutar del viaje.

Buzz Off!

Connie the horse was going on a camping trip with her family. This was her first time going out and she did not like bugs. On the first night, there were many bugs, even by the campfire. She did not like them because she hated the feeling of them biting her. She tried to get away from them and got into the tent, but they were in there too! Her mother asked her to get out of the tent, she had a spray-on repellant to keep the bugs away. Connie came out and her mother applied the repellant on her fur. The bugs no longer bothered her, and Connie began to enjoy the trip.

14 – Búsqueda de Libros

Felicity fue a la biblioteca porque necesitaba encontrar un libro para un proyecto de clase. No iba muy a menudo a las bibliotecas, ¡así que se sorprendió al ver cuántos libros había allí! No sabía cómo estaban ordenados los libros, pero estaba decidida a encontrar el libro por su cuenta. Pasó tantas horas buscando, pero se distraía fácilmente y simplemente no podía encontrar su libro. Se hizo un anuncio sobre el cierre de la biblioteca. Felicity finalmente le pidió ayuda a un bibliotecario y le dijeron dónde buscar el libro. Ella fue directamente a esa sección, con la esperanza de agarrar el libro antes de que cerraraba la biblioteca. Pero cuando llegó allí, el libro ya estaba prestado.

Book Search

Felicity went to the library because she needed to find a book for a class project. She did not go in libraries very often, so she was surprised at seeing how many books were in there! She did not know how the books were sorted, but she was determined to find the book on her own. She spent so many hours looking, but she was easily distracted and just could not find her book. An announcement was made about the library closing. Felicity finally asked a librarian for help, and they told her where to look. She went straight to that section, hoping to grab the book before the library closed. But when she got there the book was already checked out.

15 – Día de Fotos

Renee tenía que levantarse temprano en la mañana y estaba muy gruñón. Era un día de fotos en la escuela y su madre quería asegurarse de que se viera bien. No quería llevar corbata, ni peinarse hacia atrás, ni llevar zapatos elegantes. Pero su mamá le dijo que tenía que hacerlo porque su abuela quería una buena foto de él.

Cuando llegó a la escuela, él no pudo resistirse a jugar al fútbol con sus amigos. Trató de tener cuidado con su atuendo, pero tropezó y cayó en un gran charco de barro. No le dijo a su mamá y se cambió antes de que ella se enterara. Sin embargo, cuando finalmente llegaron las fotos, ¡su mamá estaba tan sorprendida! Estaba cubierto de barro en la imagen. Su abuela atesora esa imagen hasta este día.

Picture Day

Renee had to get up early in the morning, and he was very grumpy. It was picture day at school, and his mom wanted to make sure he looked just right. He did not want to wear a tie, or to comb his hair back, or to wear fancy shoes. But his mom told him he had to because his grandma wanted a good picture of him.

When he got to school, he could not resist playing soccer with his friends. He tried to be careful with his outfit, but he tripped and fell in a big puddle of mud. He did not tell his mom and got changed before she found out. However, when the pictures finally came, his mom was so surprised! He was covered in mud in the picture. His grandma treasures that picture to this day.

16 – Un Sándwich Preciado

Arlo la ardilla encontró un delicioso sándwich detrás del contenedor de basura. Tenía jamón, mayonesa, tomate y lechuga. Él estaba disfrutando de su sabrosa comida, pero Alfonso, la ardilla gorda, estaba cerca. Olió el sándwich y lo quería todo para si mismo. Arlo sabía que Alfonso era un matón y por lo general obtenía lo que quería. Arlo no sabía qué iba a hacer. De repente se oyó un ruido fuerte y entró un perro corriendo, ladrando y gruñendo. Arlo fue lo suficientemente rápido para esconderse, pero Alfonso fue perseguido por un árbol. Arlo tuvo un momento para esconder su sándwich y salió corriendo con lo suficiente para comer antes de que Alfonso pudiera regresar.

A Prized Sandwich

Arlo the squirrel found a delicious sandwich behind the dumpster. It had ham, mayo, tomato, and lettuce in it. He was enjoying his tasty meal, but Alfonso the fat squirrel was nearby. He smelled the sandwich and he wanted it all to himself. Arlo knew that Alfonso was a bully and usually got what he wanted. Arlo did not know what he was going to do. Suddenly there was a loud noise, and a dog came in running, barking, and growling. Arlo was quick enough to hide, but Alfonso got chased up a tree. Arlo had a moment to hide his sandwich and he ran off with enough to eat before Alfonso could come back.

17 – Hora de la Siesta

Vicky la serpiente vivía en un sótano. Era fresco, oscuro y tenía muchos escondites pequeños. Un día, un montón de voces la despertó de su siesta. Había humanos midiendo paredes y moviendo muebles. Esto fue un problema porque los muebles ayudaron a darle los mejores lugares para esconderse. Ella estaba de mal humor, así que se deslizó fuera para ver qué estaba pasando. La gente la vio y alguien gritó. Dejaron caer lo que sostenían y salieron corriendo del sótano. Afortunadamente, alguien apagó la luz para que ella pudiera volver a su siesta.

Nap Time

Vicky the snake lived in a basement. It was cool, dark, and it had lots of little hiding spots. One day, she was woken from her nap by a bunch of voices. There were humans measuring walls and moving furniture around. This was a problem because the furniture helped give her all the best hiding spots. She was grumpy, so she slithered out to see what was going on. The people saw her, and someone screamed. They dropped what they were holding and ran out of the basement. Luckily someone turned off the light, so she could go right back to her nap.

18 – Un Día Tranquilo, Interrumpido

Arnie el armadillo caminaba hacia su estanque favorito. En su camino, saludó a sus diversos amigos que vivían en el camino. Cuando llegó, vio que había una nueva familia. Era una madre pato con cinco patitos. Los niños estaban ocupados jugando, pero hacían mucho ruido. Arnie estaba molesto porque su rutina implicaba relajarse en este estanque y solo quería algo de paz y tranquilidad. Se acercó a hablar con los patitos y les preguntó si podían callarse. Los niños nunca habían visto un armadillo, así que se asustaron y se fueron volando antes de que él tuviera la oportunidad de hablar. Arnie estaba sorprendido, pero feliz de haber recuperado su estanque tranquilo.

A Quiet Day, Interrupted

Arnie the armadillo was walking to his favorite pond. On his way there, he said hi to his various friends that lived along the way. When he arrived, he saw there was a new family. The was a mother duck with five ducklings. The children were busy playing, but they were making so much noise. Arnie was upset because his routine involved relaxing at this pond and he just wanted some peace and quiet. He went over to talk to the ducklings to ask if they could please quiet down. The kids had never seen an armadillo, so they got scared and flew away before he even had a chance to speak. Arnie was surprised, but happy have his quiet pond back.

19 – El Concurso de Belleza

Cedrick la cebra y su hermana Selena discutieron. Ella estaba diciendo no solo que tenía más rayas que él, sino que sus rayas se veían más bonitas que las de él. Cedrick se sintió ofendido porque sabía que era la envidia de otras cebras. Discutieron hasta que decidieron que necesitaban una opinión externa. Pidieron a sus amigos y vecinos que votaran por quién tenía las rayas más bonitas del barrio. Una vez que sintieron que habían preguntado a suficientes personas, contaron los votos. ¡Fue un empate!

The Beauty Contest

Cedrick the zebra and his sister Selena got into an argument. She was saying not only that she had more stripes than him, but that her stripes looked prettier than his. Cedrick was offended because he knew he was the envy of other zebras. They argued until they decided that they needed an outside opinion. They asked their friends and neighbors for a vote to be taken for who had the prettiest stripes in the neighborhood. Once they felt they had asked enough people, they tallied up the votes. It was a tie!

20 – Todo en un Día de Trabajo

Oswal, la hormiga, tenía un día ocupado por delante. Tuvo que construir nuevos túneles y encontrar comida para su colonia. Hoy no habría tiempo para la siesta. Mientras buscaba comida, él vio que había una ventana abierta en la casa cercana. Entró y vio que había una gran bolsa de azúcar. Él hizo un agujero en él y decidió que había encontrado una mina de oro. Se apresuró al hormiguero y se lo contó a todos. Regresó con amigos y trajeron mucha azúcar a la colonia.

All in a Day's Work

Oswal the ant had a busy day ahead of him. He had to build new tunnels and find food for his colony. There would be no time for a nap today. While he was out looking for food, he saw there was an open window in the nearby house. He went inside and he saw there was a big bag of sugar. He chewed a hole into it and decided he found a gold mine. He hurried to the ant hill and told everyone all about it. He came back with friends and they brought so much sugar back to the colony.

21 – Mudarse

Connie el conejito se estaba mudando de la conejera de sus padres. No quería vivir demasiado lejos de sus padres, pero también quería demostrar que podía cuidar de sí misma. Decidió irse a vivir con amigos. Ninguno de ellos había tenido que cuidar su propia conejera antes, así que todo se puso disorganisado. Su madre decidió visitar la por sorpresa después de un mes, y le sorprendió el desorden que estaba en la conejera. Connie estaba avergonzada, pero ella culpaba a sus amigos. La mamá se echó a reír porque ya sabía que Connie estaba desordenada, pero ahora era su propio desorden para limpiar.

Moving Out

Connie the Bunny was moving out of her parents' burrow. She did not want to live too far from her parents, but she also wanted to prove she could take care of herself. She decided to move in with friends. None of them ever had to take care of their own burrow before, so it got messy. Her mom decided to have a surprise visit after a month, and she was shocked by how dirty the burrow was. Connie was embarrassed, but she blamed her friends. The mom started laughing because she already knew Connie was messy, but now it was her own mess to clean up.

22 – Demasiado Cambio

Grecia la gallina estaba muy molesta. Los granjeros le estaban quitando el gallinero y ella no tenía nada que decir. Amaba su gallinero; ella tuvo el mismo durante años. Se aseguró de chillar y picotear para que los granjeros supieran lo infeliz que estaba. Cuando se fueron, ella se instaló en el césped y se enfurruñó. Grecia se dosificó, pero los mismos granjeros luego la despertaron. ¡Habían traído un nuevo gallinero más grande! Ella corrió a investigarlo tan pronto como se instaló. ¡Tenía tanto espacio! Decidió que ya no estaba enojada con los granjeros.

Too Much Change

Grecia the chicken had her feathers ruffled. The farmers were taking away her chicken coop and she had no say in it. She loved her coop; she had the same one for years. She made sure to squawk and peck to let the farmers know how unhappy she was. When they were gone, she settled in the lawn and sulked. Grecia dosed off, but she was woken up by the same farmers. They had brought a bigger chicken coop! She ran over to investigate it as soon as it was set up. It had so much room! She decided she was no longer mad at the farmers.

23 – Andar de Travieso

La gata Gabriella se metió en la maceta e hizo un gran desorden. Pero ella no estaba preocupada, sino que estaba bastante segura de que sus humanos no descubrirían que era ella. Sin embargo, ella era hija única y estaba cubierta de tierra. Uno de sus humanos le dio un gran abrazo y la llevó al baño. La ducha estaba abierta y se dio cuenta de que estaba a punto de bañarse. No le gustaba estar mojada, así que trató de escapar. Desafortunadamente, la puerta del baño estaba cerrada, por lo que no podía viajar muy lejos. Ella ahora estaba completamente limpia, pero el baño estaba cubierto de barro. Pronto cuando Gabriela salió, corrió y se escondió en la ropa limpia.

Being Naughty

Gabriella the cat got into the flowerpot and made a big mess. She was not worried though, she was pretty sure her humans would not find out it was her. However, she was an only child, and she was covered in dirt. One of her humans gave her a big hug and carried her into the bathroom. The shower was on and she realized that she was about to have a bath. She did not like being wet, so she tried to get away. Unfortunately, the bathroom door was closed, so she could not travel far. She was fully cleaned up, but the bathroom was covered in mud. Once Gabriela was let out, she ran and hid in the clean laundry.

24 – La Hora de Máximo Tránsito

Quintin el cuervo tenía un gran día por delante. Había encontrado un arbol de nogales y sabía que romper esas cáscaras sería difícil. Se despertó temprano en la mañana y recogió tantas nueces como pudo. Luego extendió un montón de nueces por todo un camino cercano. Como se esperaba, comenzó la hora de máximo tránsito y muchos autos pasaron sobre su alijo de nueces. Miró su trabajo y vio que la mayoría de sus nueces estaban abiertas. ¿Sabes cuál fue la mejor parte de su plan? Sabía que los coches seguían un patrón basado en los semáforos de la calle. Sabía cuándo entrar para sacar sus preciadas nueces de la calle. Tuvo un gran almuerzo e incluso tuvo suficiente para compartir.

Rush Hour

Quintin the raven had a big day ahead of him. He had found walnut tree and he knew breaking those shells would be difficult. He woke up early in the morning and gathered as many walnuts as he could. Then he spread out a bunch of the walnuts all over a nearby road. As expected, rush hour began and many cars drove over his stash of nuts. He looked over his work and saw that most of his nuts were broken open. Do you know what the best part of his plan was? He knew the cars followed a pattern based on street signal lights. He knew when to come in to take his prized nuts off the street. He had a big lunch and even had enough to share.

25 – Mimarse

Petra la periquita ha estado deseando que le peinen las plumas hacia más de una semana. Fue al salón y llegó 20 minutos antes de su cita. Al final de su día de spa, sus plumas se veían hermosas, sus uñas estaban cortadas y su pico pulido. Fue a pagar y estaba más que feliz de pagar una buena propina a su estilista. Decidió mimarse aún más. De camino a casa, fue a buscar su alpiste favorito. Vio su película favorita e incluso llamó a su mejor amiga para compartir como el día era tan maravilloso. Realmente ella debería hacer esto más a menudo.

Pamper Yourself

Petra the parakeet has been looking forward to getting her feathers styled for over a week now. She went to the salon and she was 20 minutes early for her appointment. By the end of her spa day, her feathers looked beautiful, her nails were cut, and her beak was polished. She went to pay, and she was more than happy to pay a good tip for her stylist. She decided to pamper herself even further. On the way home, she went to get herself her favorite birdseed. She watched her favorite movie and she even called her best friend to share what a delightful day she had. She really should do this more often.

Section 3: Workbook Activities for Kids

The Doctor's Office

Every now and then we need to see a medical professional. Whether you feel sick, got injured, or simply are getting a check-up, you will need to learn some key words here.

El, La, Los, Las

Fill in the blanks with the correct word.

___ doctor/___ doctora – The doctor

___ medico/___ médica – The doctor

___ enfermero/___ enfermera – nurse

___ hospital – The hospital

___ sala the emergencia – emergency room

___ dolor – the pain

___ entumecimiento – the numbness

___ hormigueo – the tingling

___ corazón – the heart

___ pulmones – the lungs

___ piel – the skin

___ estómago – the stomach

___ higado – The liver

___ infección – the infection

___ tos – the cough

___ gripe – the flu

___ fiebre – the fever

___ herida – the injury

___ huesos – the bones

___ medicina – the medicine

___ asma – the asthma

Phrases

Me siento horrible	I feel awful.
Me duele aquí	It hurts here.
Duele cuando hago esto	It hurts when I do this.
No puedo moverlo	I can't move it.
Me siento mareado	I feel dizzy.
Tengo ganas de vomitar	I feel like vomiting.
Vomité 3 veces	I threw up 3 times.
Siento que me voy a desmayar -	I feel like I'm going to pass out.
Soy alérgico a huevos	I'm allergic to eggs.
Mi piel me pica mucho	My skin itches a lot.
Siento una sensación de ardor.	I feel a burning sensation.

Conjugations

For each challenge below, you will see the base verb. Try to figure out who is taking the action and what the tense of the action is. Look at the Spanish sentence and write in the correct conjugation. Use the English sentence to help you solve each problem. The first line is filled out for you (Verb translations are in bold.)

Acostar - You (formal) - Present tense

Usted puede acostarse mientras espera al médico.

You can **lay down** while you wait for the doctor.

Aguantar - __________ - ___________

No creo que puedo ________ más el dolor.

I do not think I can **tolerate** the pain any longer.

Apoyar - __________ - ___________

Esta férula _________ su brazo mientras sana.

This brace will **support** your arm while it heals.

Auscultar - __________ - ___________

Ellas ___________ mis pulmones con un estetoscopio.

They **listened** to my lungs **with a stethoscope**.

Ayunar - __________ - ___________

_________ antes de que tomemos una muestra de sangre.

You will **fast** before we take a blood sample.

Causar - __________ - ___________

¿Qué crees que _______ que la gente tosa?

What do you think **causes** people to cough?

Descansar - __________ - ___________

¿Cuál es su frecuencia cardíaca cuando está __________?

What is your heart rate when you are **resting**?

Curar - __________ - ___________

Este medicamento ________ su dolor de cabeza.

This medication will **cure** your headache.

Empeorar/Mejorar - __________ - ___________

Sus síntomas ___________ antes de que ___________.

Your symptoms will **get worse** before they **get better**.

Inhalar/Exhalar - __________ - ___________

Saqué mi inhalador y yo _______ y ________ lentamente.

I took out my inhaler and I **inhaled** and **exhaled** slowly.

Fracturar - __________ - ___________

Ella se __________ el pie mientras patinaba.

She **fractured** her foot while she was skateboarding.

Inflammar - __________ - ___________

Su codo se ________ mucho después de caer sobre él.

His elbow was very **inflamed** after he fell on it.

Recetar - __________ - ___________

Un médico deberá __________ algún medicamento.

A doctor will need to **prescribe** some medication for you.

Torcer - __________ - ___________

Se ________ la muñeca cuando jugaba voleibol.

He **sprained** his wrist when he was playing volleyball.

Temer - __________ - ___________

Yo _________ a la dentista, así que no quiero ir.

I **am afraid** of the dentist, so I do not want to go.

Visitar - __________ - ___________

Yo __________ a mi abuela enferma en el hospital.

I **visited** my sick grandma in the hospital.

Which is correct?

Circle the correct version of the word based on the context, tense, or person taking the action. Translations are provided.

¿(Hice / Hiciste) (el / la / los / las) cita con (el / la / los / las) dentista?

¿Qué medicación (estuviste / está / estar) tomando actualmente?

¿Se ha (estuviste / estado / estar) limpiando (el / la / los / las) dientes con hilo dental?

¿Le (dije / dijo / dices) a (el / la / los / las) enfermera sobre todas sus alergias?

(Reprogramaste / Reprograme) su cita en (el / la / los / las) recepción.

¿(Tenía / Tendras / Tiene) un registro que demuestre que (estuviste / estarás / está al día con todas sus vacunas?

(Enumeraste / Enumerando / Enumere) sus síntomas cuando (hablaste / hable / hablando) con su médico.

¿Usted cómo ha (estuve / estado / estados) desde su última cita?

Translation

- Did you make the dentist appointment?
- What medication are you currently taking?
- Have you been flossing your teeth?
- Did you tell the nurse about all your allergies?
- Reschedule your appointment at the front desk.
- Do you have a record proving you are you caught up with all your vaccinations?
- Please list your symptoms when you speak with your doctor.
- How have you been since your last appointment?

Taking Care of the Animals

Cats, dogs, snakes, rabbits, or even horses. We love to play with animals, we love to watch them explore and have fun. It is our responsibility to take care of them properly. We enjoy it!

Phrases

Montando un caballo — Riding a horse.

Cortar uñas — Clipping nails.

Comida húmeda o comida seca — Wet food or dry food.

Está mudando de piel — They are shedding skin.

Una cita con el veterinario — A vet appointment.

Yo tengo una cita de aseo personal

I have a grooming appointment.

¿Entrena mascotas aquí? — Do you train pets here?

¿Cuánto por una bolsa de grillos?

How much for a bag of crickets?

Almohadillas de entrenamento para perros - Dog training pads

¿Dónde está la jaula para mascotas? - Where is the pet carrier?

Esta torre de gatos se ve bonita. - This cat tower looks pretty.

Necesitamos un nuevo rascador

We need a new scratching post.

Unmix and Match

Match the Spanish phrase with the English translation. Refer to vocab from other sections and use context clues!

Alimentalos por favor	Use the laser pointer.
Cambia la caja de arena	Please feed them.
Jugar con ellos	Throw the ball!
Usa el puntero láser	Change the litter box.
Cepille su pelaje	Play with them.
Tosiendo una Bola de pelo	Brush their fur.
Dales agua	Wagging their tail.
Meneando la cola	Be careful when they hiss.
Ten cuidado cuando silban	Growling.
¡Lanza la pelota!	Coughing up a furball.
Gruñiendo	Give them water.

Conjugations

For each challenge below, you will see the base verb. Try to figure out who is taking the action and what the tense of the action is. Look at the Spanish sentence and write in the correct conjugation. Use the English sentence to help you solve each problem. (Verb translations are in bold.)

Cepillar - tu – future tense

Después de la escuela, recuerde cepillar al perro.

After school, remember to **brush** the dog.

Bañar - __________ - ___________

Ahora es tu turno de ______ al perro.

It is your turn to **bathe** the dog.

Chequear - __________ - ___________

¿___________ las patas del perro en busca de barro antes de entrar?

Did you **check** the dog's paws for mud before coming in?

Cuidar - __________ - ___________

¿Vas a _______ a los gatitos o debería hacerlo yo?

Are you going to **care** for the kittens, or should I?

Orinar - __________ - ___________

El gato _______ en la planta, no en la caja de arena.

The cat **urinated** on the plant, not the litter box.

Sudar - __________ - ___________

Los perros solo_______ por la nariz y los pies.

Dogs only **sweat** from their nose and feet.

Sentar - __________ - ___________

El gato está ________ en el alféizar de la ventana.

The cat is **sitting** on the windowsill.

Responder - __________ - ___________

El lagarto no ________ a su nombre.

The lizard does not **respond** to his name.

Pesar - __________ - ___________

¿________ al gatito antes de darle la medicación?

Did you **weigh** the kitten before giving medication?

Morder - __________ - ___________

Él fue ________ por una araña.

He was **bitten** by a spider.

Llamar - __________ - ___________

Yo ______ al veterinario para el gato Mittens.

I **called** the vet for Mittens the cat.

Which is correct?

Circle the correct version of the word based on the context, tense, or person taking the action. Translations are provided.

(Entrené / Entrenar) a mi perro para que (tocara / tocaste / tocar) una campana cada vez que necesitara (usar / usaba / usaste) el baño.

Habla con tu veterinario sobre (el / la / los / las) medicamentos contra (el / la / los / las) gusano del corazón y (el / la/ los / las) pulgas.

(Asegurar / Asegúrese) de que su mascota (tendrá / tenga / tener) los dientes limpios o se (pudrir / pudrirán / pudriste).

No (apagar / apagó / apagues) (el / la /los / las) lámpara de calor, mi lagarto la (necesita / necesitaba / necio).

Mi hermana (dejaste / dejó / dejará) que mi hámster (salio / saliera) de su jaula y yo (necesitaba / necesito) ayuda para (encontrarlo / encontrare).

(El / La / Los / Las) instrucciones y (El / La / Los / Las) comida para peces (están / estaré) justo al lado de (El / La / Los / Las) pecera.

A mi gata le (gustando / gusta) (jugaste / jugar / jugando) con las cintas, pero a veces se las (comen / comiste / comé), lo cual es malo para (él / ella / ellos / ellas).

Usted (necesito / necesitas / necesitando) (enseñaste / enseñar) a los cachorros y gatitos a (ir / van / vamos) al baño.

(El / La / Los / Las) gatos (dejaste / dejaráis / dejarán) de arañar los muebles si (están / estás / estar) entrenados para (usando / usar / usaras) un poste rascador.

Translations

- I trained my dog to ring a bell every time they need to use the restroom.
- Talk to your vet about heartworm and flea medication.
- Make sure your pet has clean teeth, or they will rot.
- Do not turn off the heat lamp, my pet lizard needs it.
- My sister let my hamster out of its cage, and I need help finding them.
- The instructions and fish food are right next to the fishbowl.
- My cat likes to play with ribbons, but sometimes they eat the ribbon, which is bad for them.
- You need to potty train puppies and kittens.
- Cats will stop clawing the furniture if they are trained to use a scratching post instead.

Working in the Garden

Garden work can be very rewarding, from watching seeds becoming sprouts, to arranging flowers and harvesting food. There is much to do with gardening!

Fill in the Blank

Can you figure out where each word belongs? If you have trouble filling in these blanks, check out the English translations after this challenge.

Word Bank

césped, macetas, hojas, segar, árbol, rastrillo, arbustos, regadera, mantilla, flores, ramas, guantes, horquilla

Plantamos este _________ cuando tenía diez años.

Acabo de terminar de ________ el césped.

Los _________ no han sido bien cuidados.

Las _______ se ven bonitas en otoño.

¿Estás aquí para reemplazar el_________?

Las _______ tienen tantos colores brillantes.

Hay un letrero que dice "Manténgase alejado del _______".

Las _______ se acercan demasiado a los cables.

Necesito ________ nuevos, estos tienen agujeros.

Regué el jardín y las __________ del porche.

Esta _______ tiene una fuga, pero no veo una grieta.

¡Mi _________ es como una horca pequeno!

¿Usaste el _________para recoger agujas de pino?

Translations

There is a sign that says, "Keep off grass."

The flowers have so many bright colors.

I need new gloves; these ones have holes in them.

I watered the garden and the pots on the porch.

This watering can is leaking, but I do not see a crack.

I hand fork is like a mini pitchfork!

Did you use the rake to pick up pine needles?

I just finished mowing the lawn.

We planted this tree when I was ten years old.

The leaves look pretty in autumn.

Are you here to replace the mulch?

The bushes have not been well cared for.

The branches are getting too close to the cables.

Mini Unmix and Match

Match the Spanish words with the English definition.

El abono	Insecticide kills destructive insects.
La carretilla	the garden hose
El herbicida	Pesticide destroys plagues in plants.
La manga	the wheelbarrow, a cart for dirt and stone.
El Insecticida	Compost nurtures plants.
El abono orgánico	Fertilizer strengthens plants.
El Plaguicida	Herbicide kills invasive verbs.

Unmix and Match

Match the Spanish words with the English definition. Use context clues and Spanish words that look similar!

La paleta	the hat, to create shade on your head.
La rastrilla	the mower, the cutter of lawns.
Lo horquilla	the spade or pointed shovel.
Las tijeras de poder	the gloves that protect your hands.
La maceta	the gardening hoe.
La regadera	the flat shovel, shaped like a plane.
Los guantes	the pruners, powerful scissors.
El sombrero	the trowel, a mini shovel.
La azada	the rake, a curved fork.
La horca	the watering can.
La pala	the hand fork, a mini pitchfork.
La pala plana	the pitchfork; a giant fork.
La cortadora	the pot that holds small plants.

Conjugations

For each challenge below, you will see the base verb. Try to figure out who is taking the action and what the tense of the action is. Look at the Spanish sentence and write in the correct conjugation. Use the English sentence to help you solve each problem. (Verb translations are in bold.)

Crecer - Ellos – present tense

Los tomates están creciendo rápidamente.

The tomatoes are **growing** quickly.

Ajardinar - __________ - ___________

Los dueños anteriores hicieron un trabajo terrible en __________ la yarda.

The previous owners did a terrible job **landscaping** the yard.

Cavar - __________ - ___________

El perro _________ muchos agujeros en la yarda delantero.

The dog **dug** a lot of holes in the front yard.

Cortar - __________ - ___________

Necesitamos ________ el árbol este fin de semana.

We need to **cut** the tree down this weekend.

Esparsar - __________ - ___________

Pedro __________ el fertilizante en el jardín.

Pedro will **spread** the fertilizer in the garden.

Plantar - __________ - ___________

Estamos _________ la calabaza junto a las zanahorias.

We are **planting** the squash next to the carrots.

Podar - __________ - ___________

¿Ya _________ las rosas?

Did you **prune** the roses yet?

Regar - __________ - ___________

Yo ya _________ las plantas hoy.

I already **watered** the plants today.

Recoger - __________ - ___________

Yo _____________ los recortes esta tarde.

I will **pick up** the clippings this afternoon.

Rastrillar - __________ - ___________

Hay que _________ las hojas antes de que llegue tu tío.

The leaves need to be **raked** before your uncle arrives.

Segar - __________ - ___________

Ella _________ el césped cada dos sábados.

She **mows** the grass every other Saturday.

Which is correct?

Circle the correct version of the word based on the context, tense, or person taking the action. Translations are provided.

No (regaste / riegue) demasiado (el / las / los / la) plantas porque se (ahogaste / ahogarán / ahogar).

(Recordando / Recuerde / Recordadora) quitar las malas hierbas del jardín o no (crecer / crecerán / creciste) bien.

¿(Necesitas / Necesitando) latices para (sosteniendo / sostener / sostena) tus enredaderas de tomate?

Puede (utilisaste / utilizando / utilizer) el abono procesado cuando (configure / configurar / confiaste) su jardín.

¿Usted (etiquetando / etique / etiquetó) cada una de las semillas que (plantaste/ plantaras / plantó?

(Mantener / Mantenga / Manteniste) a (el/ la/ los / las) perros fuera del jardín y (teniste / tendras / tenga) cuidado con las plagas.

¿(El / La / Los / Las) sandías ya (estuviste / estas / están) listas para ser (recolectando / recolectadas)?

Translations

- Do not overwater the plants because they will drown.
- Please remember to weed the garden, or they will not grow well.
- Do you need latices to support your tomato vines?
- You can use the processed compost when you set up your garden.
- Did you label each of the seeds that you planted?
- Keep dogs out of the garden and watch out for pests.
- Are the watermelons ready to be harvested yet?

Helping in the Kitchen

All kinds of tasty creations come from a kitchen. Do you sometimes like to help make cookies, a sandwich, or even a cake? Let us figure out what we need to know to help cook, in Spanish!

Fill in the Blank

Can you figure out where each word belongs? If you have trouble filling in these blanks, check out the English translations after this challenge.

Word bank

Refrigerador – Licuadora – Microondas – Horno – Mezclador

Congelador – Lavaplatos – Cafetera – Horno Tostador

Freidora – Tostadora – Multiprocesadora

El ______________ es un gran lugar para guardar las sobras, así como la leche, los huevos y otras delicias.

El ______________ es un lugar para almacenar alimentos congelados y cubitos de hielo.

Puede utilizar el ___________ para preparar una comida rápida, pero tenga cuidado de no poner ningún metal en su interior.

El _________ es ideal para todas sus necesidades de horneado y asado. Puede hacer magdalenas, pavo y lasaña.

La __________ es ideal para tostar bien el pan, entre otras cosas sabrosas.

El ________ ________es como un mini horno que se coloca sobre la encimera.

La ___________ cocina por circular aire muy caliente sobre la comida.

La ___________ puede hacer deliciosos batidos de frutas y salsas picantes.

La _____________ puede ayudar a mezclar los ingredientes al hacer pasteles y crema batida.

El _________________ puede ayudarlo a cortar y picar ingredientes como tomates, cebollas y pimientos.

Puedes ahorrar tiempo lavando los platos si tiene un ___________.

Una ___________ puede usar posos de café para hacer una infusión caliente.

Translations:

- A refrigerator is a great place to store your leftovers as well as your milk your eggs and other tasty treats.
- The freezer is a place to store frozen items and ice cubes.
- You can use the microwave to prepare a quick meal but be careful not to put any metal inside it.
- The oven is great for all your baking and roasting needs. It can make cupcakes, Turkey, and lasagna.
- A toaster is great for well toasting bread among other tasty things.
- A toaster oven is like a mini oven that sits on your counter.
- An air fryer cooks by circulating really hot air over your food.
- A blender can make tasty fruit smoothies and spicy salsas.
- A mixer can help mix ingredients when you make cakes and whipped cream.
- A food processor can help you slice and dice ingredients like tomatoes, onions, and peppers.
- You can save times washing your dishes if you have a dishwasher.
- A coffee maker can use coffee grounds to make a hot brew.

Conjugations

For each challenge below, you will see the base verb. Try to figure out who is taking the action and what the tense of the action is. Look at the Spanish sentence and write in the correct conjugation. Use the English sentence to help you solve each problem. The first line is filled out for you (Verb translations are in bold.)

Apagar – You – Past tense

Antes de ponerse cómodo, ¿Apagasté el horno?

Before you get comfortable, did you **turn off** the oven?

Batir - ___________ - ____________

Después de este paso necesitaremos __________ la masa.

After this step we will need to **mix** the batter.

Beber - ___________ - ____________

¿Has ___________ refrescos hoy?

Have you been **drinking** soda today?

Calentar - ___________ - ____________

Te he ____________ más tortillas.

I have **heated up** some more tortillas for you.

Cenar - ___________ - ____________

Esta noche ___________ con los vecinos.

This evening we will be **dining** with the neighbors.

Cocinar - ___________ - ____________

Ellos estan ____________ algo especial para nosotros.

They are cooking something special for us.

Disfrutar - ___________ - ____________

Realmente estoy ___________ este batido.

I am really **enjoying** this smoothie.

Gustar - ___________ - ____________

Espero que les ________ mucho la enchilada que hice.

I hope you guys really **like** the enchilada that I made.

Hacer - ___________ - ____________

Necesito tu ayuda para _____ galletas y pan de plátano hoy.

I need your help **making** cookies and banana bread today.

Lavar - ___________ - ____________

¿Ya ________ los platos?

Did you **wash** the dishes yet?

Limpiar - ___________ - ____________

Por favor __________ el desorden en el microondas.

Please **clean** the mess in the microwave.

Masticar - ___________ - ____________

Por favor _________ con la boca cerrada.

Please **chew** with your mouth closed.

Mezclar - __________ - ___________

¿Qué haces después de ________ los ingredientes secos?

What do you do after **mixing** the dry ingredients?

Oler - __________ - ___________

¿Has ______ alguna vez extracto de vainilla?

Have you ever **smelt** vanilla extract?

Preparar - __________ - ___________

_________ huevos y tocino para el desayuno.

I will be **preparing** eggs and bacon for breakfast.

Quemar - __________ - ___________

¿Algo se ________? ¿Hay algo en el horno?

Is something **burning**? Is something in the oven?

Tapar - __________ - ___________

Baja el fuego y _____ la olla.

Lower the heat and **cover** the pot.

Which is correct?

Circle the correct version of the word based on the context, tense, or person taking the action. Translations are provided.

La temperatura de (el / la / los / las) mantequilla es importante para (horneando / hornear). (Conozi / Conozca / Conoces) (el / la / los / las) diferencia entre ablandado, frío y derretido.

(Sigues / Seguiste / Siga) la receta lo más posible a (el / la / los / las) hora de hornear. (El / La / Los / Las) más mínimo cambio puede (alteriste / alterar) la textura de la masa.

¿Sabes (mediendo / mediste / medir) (el / la / los / las) ingredientes? ¿(Conoce / Conosiste) la diferencia entre cucharadita, cucharada y todas (el / la / los / las) fracciones involucradas?

Debe (usando / usar / usaste) (un / una / unos / unas) termómetro para medir la temperatura en la parte más fría de la comida, especialmente cuando (cocina / cocinar) carne.

¡(Mantiene / Mantenga) el horno cerrado! (Estamos / Estás) dejando entrar (el / la / los / las) aire frío cada vez que (mirando / miras / miraste) dentro.

Aunque sacó (el / la / los / las) comida del horno, todavía (estar / está / estamos) lo suficientemente caliente como para (cocinarse / cocinando).

Translations

- The temperature of the butter is important in baking. Know the difference between softened, chilled, and melted.
- Follow the recipe as possible when it comes to baking. The slightest change can change the texture of the pastry.
- Do you know how to measure ingredients? Do you know the difference between teaspoon, tablespoon, and all the fractions involved?
- You should use a thermometer to measure the temperature at the coldest part of the food, especially when you cook meat.
- Keep the oven closed! You are letting the cold air in every time you peek inside.
- Even though you took the food out of the oven, it is still hot enough that it is still cooking.

Caring for the Car

Would you want to help with taking care of the family car? Let us find out what basic tools you need to use and what actions you will need to do to take care of the car.

Which is correct?

Circle the correct version of the word based on the context, tense, or person taking the action. Translations are provided.

Necesita (cambiar / cambiando / cambio) su aceite cada tres mil millas, o cada tres meses.

Yo siempre (cambiando / cambiar / cambio) los filtros de aire al menos una vez al año.

(Las /Los) correas y (las / los) mangueras deben (reemplazarse / reemplazo) cuando están agrietadas o dañadas.

Debe (revise / revisar / revisando) el líquido limpiaparabrisas todos (el / la / los / las) meses.

Puede (verificar / verificare / verificando? los niveles de líquido de la transmisión con (un / una / unos / unas) varilla medidora.

(Prestando / Preste) atención a las etiquetas de advertencia, algunos fluidos (era / están / siendo) bajo presión cuando el motor está caliente.

¿(Sabías / Sabías / Saber) que la presión de los neumáticos baja cuando la temperatura exterior (soy / estaria / es) fría?

(El / La / Los / Las) líquido de frenos (ayudiendo / ayuda / ayudaste) a que su automóvil se detenga más rápidamente.

El líquido de dirección asistida (Ayudando / ayudar / ayuda) a su automóvil a girar las ruedas cuando (conduciendo / conduce / conduciste).

Debe (revisaste / revisar / revista) la banda de rodadura de sus neumáticos para (asegurarse / asegurando), de que tenga una buena tracción.

(Recuerde / Recordaste / Recordar) (llevar / llavaste / lleve) su aceite a un centro de recolección después de (un / una / unos) cambio de aceite.

No (cruciste / cruce / crusando) (un /unas / las/ los) cables cuando utilice cables de puente para (encender / endendiste) una batería.

Translations

You need to have your oil changed ever three thousand miles, or every three months.

I always change the air filters at least once a year.

Belts and hoses need to be replaced when they are cracked or damaged.

You need to check your windshield washer fluid every month.

You can check your transmission fluid levels with a dipstick.

Pay attention to warning labels, some fluids are under pressure when the engine is hot.

Did you know that tire pressure goes down when the temperature is cold outside?

Brake fluid helps your car stop more quickly.

Power steering fluid helps your car turn the wheels when you steer.

You should check the tread on your tires to make sure you have good traction.

Remember to take your oil to a collection center after an oil change.

Do not cross wires when you use jumper cables to start a battery.

Fill in the Blank
Wordbank

Destornillador (screwdriver), alicates (pliers), llaves (wrenches), trinquete y vasos (rachet and sockets), martillo (hammer), gato (jack), rampas (ramps), bandeja de aceite (oil pan), fusibles (fuses), taladro (drill), tuercas y tornillos (nuts and bolts), batería (battery), manual de servicio.

Trate de recoger todo el aceite con el ________ __ _______.

Traiga los _________ adicionales del garaje.

Este _____________ es demasiado pequeño, trae el más grande.

Necesitará los ______________ para abrirla.

Traje _________ para tamaños métricos.

Tendremos que levantar el coche con el ________.

Conduce el coche por las _______ y pon el freno de mano.

Consulte el ___________ ___ __________ para ver qué utiliza este automóvil.

Tengo _________ _ ________ para todos los tamaños.

¿Qué tipo de __________ trajiste?

El ___________ nos ayudará a trabajar más rápido.

No pierda las _________ _ ___________, los necesitaremos más adelante.

Esta __________ está muy débil y necesita ser reemplazada.

Translations

Bring the extra fuses from the garage.

This screwdriver is too small, bring the biggest one.

You will need the pliers to open it.

I brought wrenches for metric sizes.

We will have to lift the car with the jack.

Drive the car down the ramps and set the parking brake.

Check the service manual to see what this car uses.

I have ratchet and socket set for all sizes.

What kind of hammer did you bring?

The drill will help us to work faster.

Do not lose the nuts and bolts, we will need them later.

This battery is very weak and needs to be replaced.

Conjugations

For each challenge below, you will see the base verb. Try to figure out who is taking the action and what the tense of the action is. Look at the Spanish sentence and write in the correct conjugation. Use the English sentence to help you solve each problem. (Verb translations are in bold.)

Lavar - He - Present

Él está lavando nuestros dos coches.

He is **washing** both of our cars.

Encerar - ___________ - ____________

Si _____________ el camión, haré la cena.

If you **wax** the truck, I will make dinner.

Aspirar - ___________ - ____________

Ella está ___________ el interior del coche.

She is **vacuuming** the inside of the car.

Inflar - ___________ - ____________

También __________ sus llantas mientras cambian tu aceite.

They will also **inflate** your tires while you get an oil change.

Cambiar - ___________ - ____________

El aceite debe ___________ cada diez mil millas.

The oil needs to be **changed** every ten thousand miles.

Rotar - ___________ - ____________

¿Cuándo fue la última vez que le __________ los neumáticos?

When did you last have your tires **rotated**?

Pulir - __________ - ___________

Estamos _________ el rasguño en la puerta después del almuerzo.

We are **buffing** out the scratch on the door after lunch.

Limpiar - __________ - ___________

Usted ________ las ventanas con la escobilla de goma.

You **wipe** the windows with the squeegee.

Raspar - __________ - ___________

Levántese más temprano para poder ________ el hielo del parabrisas.

Wake up earlier so you can **scrape** ice off the windshield.

Conducir - __________ - ___________

Esta es la primera vez que _______ a campo traviesa.

This is her first time **driving** cross country.

Frenar - __________ - ___________

No ________ con demasiada fuerza cuando haya hielo en la carretera.

Do not **brake** too hard when there is ice on the road.

Girar - __________ - ___________

Deberá ________ a la derecha en la tercera señal de alto.

You will need to **turn** right at the third stop sign.

Señalar - __________ - ___________

Jason siempre ________ antes de girar.

Jason always **signals** before making any turn.

Learning a new language is a challenging, but very fulfilling task. Choose to learn Spanish specifically and you will see the advantages of pursuing a language that has a global presence. Spanish immersion opportunities are easy to find, and you will gain a new asset for most any career path you pursue.

Once you have learned the language, you will have access to learning a variety of Latin cultures and traditions in a far more engaging setting. You can perhaps explore recent news about Latin icons and celebrities from Spanish sources. You can partake in cultural events such as Day of the Dead in Oaxaca. You can immerse with the local population in your next vacation to Havana. You can pursue a lifelong dream of becoming an Alpaca farmer deep in the Andes Mountains in Ecuador. Really the sky is the limit when it comes to finding ways to put a new language to use.

You will find that Spanish is very easy to learn. We already share the same alphabet and there are only a couple new sounds you will need to learn to produce. Everything else will feel familiar enough to give you a solid place to start any lesson. Granted that some rules might seem tricky at first, but if you could learn English just fine, I am confident that you will be able to master the Spanish language as well.

Learning Spanish is best done through practice and through seeing it in practice. Learn the fundamentals of the language through three distinct sections in this book:

- Vocabulary and Grammar
- Short stories for Beginners
- Workbook Activities for Kids

You will learn the essential vocabulary and the basics of grammar by analyzing it in typical interactions from shopping to dining out. Learn about conjugating different types of verbs, properly marking stressed syllables, and differentiating between words that look or sound similar.

Become familiar with and learn to avoid the common pitfalls of learners that are studying Spanish as a second language. Explore the nuances of grammar in a fun and friendly setting.

This book provides a wealth of relatable and silly short stories, along with translations, to help further your understanding of the language as it is used. Learn about Petra the parakeet as she has a spa day. Learn about what is bothering Grecia the chicken and what she is worried about. Learn with Connie the bunny about what it means to move out from home. 25 stories contain a range of experiences and situations that put your vocabulary skills to work. Compare the same story in both English and Spanish and expand on your vocabulary and grammar skills.

Workbook activities for kids are also provided to put your knowledge to the test in a variety of common settings ranging from the doctor's office to the home kitchen. Pick up even more vocabulary here and solidify your knowledge on conjugations. Challenge yourself to use context clues to fill in the blanks on topics you are familiar with, and more!

www.ingramcontent.com/pod-product-compliance
Lightning Source LLC
Chambersburg PA
CBHW070315190726
48291CB00013B/1583

* 9 7 8 1 9 1 3 7 1 0 6 9 9 *